COME AND SEE

A 45 day journey with Jesus through the book of John

Name: _____

Start Date: _____

Person doing the challenge with: _____

45 Day Checklist:

1 ☐	2 ☐	3 ☐	4 ☐	5 ☐	6 ☐	7 ☐	8 ☐	9 ☐
10 ☐	11 ☐	12 ☐	13 ☐	14 ☐	15 ☐	16 ☐	17 ☐	18 ☐
19 ☐	20 ☐	21 ☐	22 ☐	23 ☐	24 ☐	25 ☐	26 ☐	27 ☐
28 ☐	29 ☐	30 ☐	31 ☐	32 ☐	33 ☐	34 ☐	35 ☐	36 ☐
37 ☐	38 ☐	39 ☐	40 ☐	41 ☐	42 ☐	43 ☐	44 ☐	45 ☐

Content

Come and See

When you read through the Gospel of John, you see Jesus inviting people to himself over and over. He didn't force himself on anyone or try to manipulate anyone into following him, he invited them to *Come and See*. Those Jesus invited invited others to *Come and See*. Eventually twelve men responded to Jesus' next invitation of "come and follow me."

You are invited to *Come and See* Jesus through the Gospel of John over the next 45 days. This is something anyone can do whether you consider yourself a follower of Jesus or not. *Come and See*, no strings attached. My prayer is that as you get to know about Jesus through reading John's Gospel you will come to know him, leave your old life behind, and say yes to his next invitation, "come and follow me."

The 45 Day Challenge

Few things will have a greater impact on your life than developing the habit of reading God's Word and spending time in prayer every day. Most likely this not drasticly change your life overnight. Slowly however God will use this daily time with him to change you from the inside out. It's sort of like changing your diet. You don't notice any drastic changes right away, but if you consistenly committed to small changes you would look and feel different six months from now.

The challenge of *Come and See* is to read through the Gospel of John and pray for 45 consecutive days. Each day you will read a new story about Jesus and be given an opportunity to interact with it, pray, and make a plan for doing the same thing the next day.

Tips for Success

1) Make the 45 day commitment. Write it down and tell someone you're doing it.

2) Do it first thing each day if possible. Use a paper Bible and not your phone because it will be less distracting.

3) Shoot for consistency over quantity. If five minutes is all you have that day, just do five minutes.

4) Keep your chart visible and put it in a place where you will see it every day.

5) Plan ahead. Anticipate upcoming challenges and make a plan to overcome them. Write down the day before when you are going to do it.

6) Invite a friend to join you on this 45 day challenge.

Bible Study Method: Engage the Text

This is a simple method that helps you get more out of what you read. Writing things down, asking questions and thinking of what you want to tell others uses more parts of your brain that just reading. If you write down a few simple things each day it will help you remember what you read and start to apply it to your life.

Engage the Text With These Four Questions

1. What does this passage tell me about Jesus? *You don't have to write down everything, but list a few things you learned about Jesus in the passage.*

2. What questions do I have about this passage? *Is there something you don't understand what's going on makes you want to know more. Jesus' favorite way of helping people learn was using questions.*

3. What verse or phrase do I want to remember and think about today?

4. What did I read today I want to share with someone else?

Prayer Method: Lord's Prayer

Jesus' disciples observed how he prayed and then asked him, "Lord, teach us to pray." Jesus' disciples had been praying for most of their lives but when they saw Jesus pray they knew something was different. They wanted to pray the way he prayed. It's ok to feel like you don't know where to go with prayer. For the first 14 days you will learn to pray how Jesus taught his disciples to pray when they asked him, "Lord, teach us to pray."

"Our Father in heaven, hallowed be your name. Your kingdom come, your will be done, on earth as it is in heaven. Give us this day our daily bread, and forgive us our debts, as we also have forgiven our debtors. And lead us not into temptation, but deliver us from evil."

The beauty of the Lord's Prayer is that it begins by taking our attention off of ourselves and our own desires and needs and centers it instead on God. You should not be the center of your prayer life, God should. Here is a simple pattern taken from the Lord's prayer you can follow.

1.   Pray for God's priorities first. *"Your kingdom come, your will be done..."*
2.   Pray for your own needs. *"Daily bread and forgive us our debts"*
3.   Pray for the strength to forgive others. *"Forgive us as we forgive others."*
4.   Pray for the strength to overcome temptation. *"Lead us not into temptation."*

The WORD Became Flesh

Day 1: John 1:1-18

John 1:1-18 is the prologue of John's letter. A prologue is an introduction that sets the scene and introduces the major themes that will be explored. John's Gospel presents Jesus not just as a prophet, but as the eternal Son of God incarnate (God in the flesh).

1) What does this passage tell me about Jesus?

_____

_____

_____

_____

_____

_____

2) What questions do I have about this passage?

_____

_____

_____

_____

_____

_____

3) What verse or phrase do I want to remember and think about today?

Interesting Fact-John begins his Gospel in a way that echoes Genesis 1:1, "In the beginning…" John calls Jesus "the Word" which in Greek is *logos*. The Greeks used *logos* to refer to an impersonal force that gave order to the universe. John tells his readers that it is the person of Jesus Christ, God incarnate, that gives reason and order to the universe, not an "impersonal force."[1]

4) What did I read today that I want to share with someone else?

_____

_____

_____

_____

_____

"Lord teach us to pray"

Our Father in heaven, hallowed be your name.
Your kingdom come, your will be done,
on earth as it is in heaven. Give us this day our daily bread,
and forgive us our debts, as we also have forgiven our debtors.
And lead us not into temptation, but deliver us from evil.

1) Pray for God's priorities first.
2) Pray for your needs: Provision and Forgiveness.
3) Pray for the strength to forgive others.
4) Pray for the strength to overcome temptation.

Time / Plan for tomorrow:

John the Baptist

Day 2: John 1:19-34

John the Baptist was the prophet whose main job was to let everyone know that the Messiah, or "The Christ," was coming. John sees Jesus and identifies him as the Messiah who had come to redeem the whole world.

1) What does this passage tell me about Jesus?

_____

_____

_____

_____

_____

2) What questions do I have about this passage?

_____

_____

_____

_____

3) What verse or phrase do I want to remember and think about today?

John the Baptist was Jesus' cousin. He was a wild man who lived on the outskirts of society, wore camel skin shirts, and had a diet of locusts and honey.

4) What did I read today that I want to share with someone else?

_____

_____

_____

_____

_____

"Lord teach us to pray"

Our Father in heaven, hallowed be your name.
Your kingdom come, your will be done,
on earth as it is in heaven. Give us this day our daily bread,
and forgive us our debts, as we also have forgiven our debtors.
And lead us not into temptation, but deliver us from evil.

1) Pray for God's priorities first.
2) Pray for your needs: Provision and Forgiveness.
3) Pray for the strength to forgive others.
4) Pray for the strength to overcome temptation.

Time / Plan for tomorrow:

Jesus Calls His First Disciples
Day 3: John 1:35-51

Jesus starts his public ministry by calling disciples. Those Jesus called left what they were doing and followed him because they believed he was the Messiah. They referred to Jesus as "rabbi" which means teacher. It was a great honor to be a disciple of a rabbi.

1) What does this passage tell me about Jesus?

2) What questions do I have about this passage?

3) What verse or phrase do I want to remember and think about today?

Philip, Nathaniel, Peter, Andrew and John were all from the same small fishing village of Bethsaida which most likely had a population smaller than Spofford, NH. It's also a good chance they were teenagers in this story.

4) What did I read today that I want to share with someone else?

_____

_____

_____

_____

_____

"Lord teach us to pray"

Our Father in heaven, hallowed be your name.
Your kingdom come, your will be done,
on earth as it is in heaven. Give us this day our daily bread,
and forgive us our debts, as we also have forgiven our debtors.
And lead us not into temptation, but deliver us from evil.

1) Pray for God's priorities first.
2) Pray for your needs: Provision and Forgiveness.
3) Pray for the strength to forgive others.
4) Pray for the strength to overcome temptation.

Time / Plan for tomorrow:

Jesus' First Public Miracle

Day 4: John 2:1-11

This was the first sign or miracle that Jesus performed.
A sign was a miracle that pointed to Jesus' identity as the Messiah and
Son of God. The purpose of a sign was to create faith in unbelievers.

1) What does this passage tell me about Jesus?

_____

_____

_____

_____

_____

_____

2) What questions do I have about this passage?

_____

_____

_____

_____

_____

3) What verse or phrase do I want to remember and think about today?

John tells us that turning water into wine was Jesus' first sign or miracle. This implies that he did not do any miracles during his childhood or teenage years, as some traditions believe.

4) What did I read today that I want to share with someone else?

_____

_____

_____

_____

_____

"Lord teach us to pray"

Our Father in heaven, hallowed be your name.
Your kingdom come, your will be done,
on earth as it is in heaven. Give us this day our daily bread,
and forgive us our debts, as we also have forgiven our debtors.
And lead us not into temptation, but deliver us from evil.

1) Pray for God's priorities first.
2) Pray for your needs: Provision and Forgiveness.
3) Pray for the strength to forgive others.
4) Pray for the strength to overcome temptation.

Time / Plan for tomorrow:

Jesus Cleanses the Temple

Day 5: John 2:12-25

This is Jesus' first major encounter with the Jewish authorities. It was a common practice to sell oxen, sheep and pigeons during Passover because people traveled a long way to Jerusalem. This saved them from having to transport animals for the sacrifice. What made Jesus upset was that they had turned an area of the temple reserved for the worship of gentiles into a marketplace, disrupting their worship of God and obstructing the very purpose of the temple.

1) What does this passage tell me about Jesus?

_____

_____

_____

_____

_____

_____

_____

2) What questions do I have about this passage?

_____

_____

_____

_____

_____

_____

3) What verse or phrase do I want to remember and think about today?

Passover is the oldest Jewish holiday celebrated. The first Passover, when the Israelites left Egypt, was almost 3,500 years ago.

4) What did I read today that I want to share with someone else?

_____

_____

_____

_____

_____

"Lord teach us to pray"

Our Father in heaven, hallowed be your name.
Your kingdom come, your will be done,
on earth as it is in heaven. Give us this day our daily bread,
and forgive us our debts, as we also have forgiven our debtors.
And lead us not into temptation, but deliver us from evil.

1) Pray for God's priorities first.
2) Pray for your needs: Provision and Forgiveness.
3) Pray for the strength to forgive others.
4) Pray for the strength to overcome temptation.

Time / Plan for tomorrow:

Jesus and Nicodemus

Day 6: John 3:1-21

Jesus meets with Nicodemus, a member of the Jewish Sanhedrin, and stresses to him the need to be "born again." Being "born again" refers to a spiritual rebirth obtained at salvation. Jesus reveals to Nicodemus that he is the Son of God sent to save the world from their sins.

1) What does this passage tell me about Jesus?

_____

_____

_____

_____

_____

_____

2) What questions do I have about this passage?

_____

_____

_____

_____

_____

3) What verse or phrase do I want to remember and think about today?

Nicodemus was one of two people who had the courage to ask Pilate for Jesus' body after his death so he could receive a proper burial.

4) What did I read today that I want to share with someone else?

_____

_____

_____

_____

_____

"Lord teach us to pray"

Our Father in heaven, hallowed be your name.
Your kingdom come, your will be done,
on earth as it is in heaven. Give us this day our daily bread,
and forgive us our debts, as we also have forgiven our debtors.
And lead us not into temptation, but deliver us from evil.

1) Pray for God's priorities first.
2) Pray for your needs: Provision and Forgiveness.
3) Pray for the strength to forgive others.
4) Pray for the strength to overcome temptation.

Time / Plan for tomorrow:

He Must Increase, I Must Decrease
Day 7: John 3:22-36

John the Baptist continues to explain to his disciples that he is not the long awaited Messiah. He is only the one chosen to get people ready for him. He likens his role to a best man at a wedding. The best man's job is to draw attention to the bridegroom, not himself.

1) What does this passage tell me about Jesus?

_____

_____

_____

_____

_____

_____

2) What questions do I have about this passage?

_____

_____

_____

_____

_____

3) What verse or phrase do I want to remember and think about today?

Baptism of repentance, the type that John the Baptist was performing, was to be done in a river with moving water because it symbolized the washing and carrying away of sin.

4) What did I read today that I want to share with someone else?

_____

_____

_____

_____

_____

"Lord teach us to pray"

> *Our Father in heaven, hallowed be your name.*
> *Your kingdom come, your will be done,*
> *on earth as it is in heaven. Give us this day our daily bread,*
> *and forgive us our debts, as we also have forgiven our debtors.*
> *And lead us not into temptation, but deliver us from evil.*

1) Pray for God's priorities first.
2) Pray for your needs: Provision and Forgiveness.
3) Pray for the strength to forgive others.
4) Pray for the strength to overcome temptation.

Time / Plan for tomorrow:

Jesus and the Samaritan Woman

Day 8: John 4:1-45

Jesus left Judea and departed for his hometown of Galilee. This journey required you to either travel through Samaria, which was shorter, or take a much longer route on the other side of the Jordan River. Most observant Jews would rather take the longer trip because they wanted nothing to do with the Samaritans. Jesus broke all sorts of "rules" by both traveling through Samaria and drinking from a Samaritan woman's water pitcher.

1) What does this passage tell me about Jesus?

2) What questions do I have about this passage?

3) What verse or phrase do I want to remember and think about today?

Sychar, the town in Samaria that Jesus and his disciples stopped in, was the place where the Old Testament Patriarch Joseph was buried.

4) What did I read today that I want to share with someone else?

_____

_____

_____

_____

_____

"Lord teach us to pray"

Our Father in heaven, hallowed be your name.
Your kingdom come, your will be done,
on earth as it is in heaven. Give us this day our daily bread,
and forgive us our debts, as we also have forgiven our debtors.
And lead us not into temptation, but deliver us from evil.

1) Pray for God's priorities first.
2) Pray for your needs: Provision and Forgiveness.
3) Pray for the strength to forgive others.
4) Pray for the strength to overcome temptation.

Time / Plan for tomorrow:

Jesus Heals the Official's Son

Day 9: John 4:46-54

The official that Jesus meets is most likely a gentile centurion (soldier) who is in the service of Herod Antipas. John is showing that Jesus is bringing the gospel to the whole world by highlighting Jesus' interactions with Nicodemus, who was a respected Jewish teacher, a Samaritan woman who was a societal outcast, and now to a soldier working for the Roman government.[2]

1) What does this passage tell me about Jesus?

2) What questions do I have about this passage?

3) What verse or phrase do I want to remember and think about today?

4) What did I read today that I want to share with someone else?

_____

_____

_____

_____

_____

"Lord teach us to pray"

Our Father in heaven, hallowed be your name.
Your kingdom come, your will be done,
on earth as it is in heaven. Give us this day our daily bread,
and forgive us our debts, as we also have forgiven our debtors.
And lead us not into temptation, but deliver us from evil.

1) Pray for God's priorities first.
2) Pray for your needs: Provision and Forgiveness.
3) Pray for the strength to forgive others.
4) Pray for the strength to overcome temptation.

Time / Plan for tomorrow:

Jesus Heals on the Sabbath

Day 10: John 5:1-18

Local legend held that the pool of Bethseda contained healing powers. The belief was that when the water was "stirred up," the first one in would be healed. This is why the pool was surrounded by the sick and lame. Jesus showed compassion on the sick man and healed him with a word.

1) What does this passage tell me about Jesus?

_____

_____

_____

_____

_____

_____

2) What questions do I have about this passage?

_____

_____

_____

_____

_____

3) What verse or phrase do I want to remember and think about today?

The Jewish Sabbath was the 7th day of the week (Saturday).
All work was forbidden on the Sabbath because in creation God
worked for 6 days and on the 7th he rested.

4) What did I read today that I want to share with someone else?

_____

_____

_____

_____

_____

"Lord teach us to pray"

Our Father in heaven, hallowed be your name.
Your kingdom come, your will be done,
on earth as it is in heaven. Give us this day our daily bread,
and forgive us our debts, as we also have forgiven our debtors.
And lead us not into temptation, but deliver us from evil.

1) Pray for God's priorities first.
2) Pray for your needs: Provision and Forgiveness.
3) Pray for the strength to forgive others.
4) Pray for the strength to overcome temptation.

Time / Plan for tomorrow:

The Authority of Jesus

Day 11: John 5:19-47

The Jews are seeking to kill Jesus because by calling God his Father he was not only claiming a unique relationship with God but also claiming equality with God. This passage helps you understand the nature of the Trinity (one God in three distinct persons) because in it we see God the Father and God the Son as separate but equal.

1) What does this passage tell me about Jesus?

2) What questions do I have about this passage?

3) What verse or phrase do I want to remember and think about today?

4) What did I read today that I want to share with someone else?

_____

_____

_____

_____

_____

"Lord teach us to pray"

Our Father in heaven, hallowed be your name.
Your kingdom come, your will be done,
on earth as it is in heaven. Give us this day our daily bread,
and forgive us our debts, as we also have forgiven our debtors.
And lead us not into temptation, but deliver us from evil.

1) Pray for God's priorities first.

2) Pray for your needs: Provision and Forgiveness.

3) Pray for the strength to forgive others.

4) Pray for the strength to overcome temptation.

Time / Plan for tomorrow:

Jesus Feeds the 5,000

Day 12: John 6:1-21

Large crowds had come to hear Jesus preach because they both saw and heard about the miracles he was performing. It was the Jewish Passover and there would have been over 100,000 additional Jews in the Jerusalem area who traveled there to celebrate. The people perceived Jesus' miracle of multiplying the bread as fulfilling the Old Testament prediction of the coming of a prophet like Moses, who fed their ancestors with manna.

1) What does this passage tell me about Jesus?

_____

_____

_____

_____

_____

_____

_____

2) What questions do I have about this passage?

_____

_____

_____

_____

_____

3) What verse or phrase do I want to remember and think about today?

Barley loaves were a staple food for poor people and the fish Jesus multiplied were most likely dried or preserved, or possibly pickled.[3]

4) What did I read today that I want to share with someone else?

_____

_____

_____

_____

_____

"Lord teach us to pray"

Our Father in heaven, hallowed be your name.
Your kingdom come, your will be done,
on earth as it is in heaven. Give us this day our daily bread,
and forgive us our debts, as we also have forgiven our debtors.
And lead us not into temptation, but deliver us from evil.

1) Pray for God's priorities first.
2) Pray for your needs: Provision and Forgiveness.
3) Pray for the strength to forgive others.
4) Pray for the strength to overcome temptation.

Time / Plan for tomorrow:

I am the Bread of Life

Day 13: John 6:22-59

This is the first of the seven "I AM" statements of Jesus recorded in the Gospel of John. Each of these statements is a claim to deity and points out a unique aspect of the satisfaction Jesus offers. Jesus, as the Bread of Life, satisfies and nourishes the deep hunger of people's souls.

1) What does this passage tell me about Jesus?

_____

_____

_____

_____

_____

_____

_____

2) What questions do I have about this passage?

_____

_____

_____

_____

_____

_____

3) What verse or phrase do I want to remember and think about today?

In Exodus 3:14 God reveals his name to Moses as "I AM WHO I AM."
This is where the Hebrew name for God, "Yahweh," comes from.

4) What did I read today that I want to share with someone else?

_____

_____

_____

_____

_____

"Lord teach us to pray"

Our Father in heaven, hallowed be your name.
Your kingdom come, your will be done,
on earth as it is in heaven. Give us this day our daily bread,
and forgive us our debts, as we also have forgiven our debtors.
And lead us not into temptation, but deliver us from evil.

1) Pray for God's priorities first.
2) Pray for your needs: Provision and Forgiveness.
3) Pray for the strength to forgive others.
4) Pray for the strength to overcome temptation.

Time / Plan for tomorrow:

The Words of Eternal Life

Day 14: John 6:60-71

Many of Jesus' disciples are offended by the hardness of his teaching and walk away. Peter and the rest of the twelve refuse to leave because they have come to believe that Jesus is the long awaited Messiah and that he held the words of eternal life.

1) What does this passage tell me about Jesus?

_____

_____

_____

_____

_____

_____

2) What questions do I have about this passage?

_____

_____

_____

_____

_____

3) What verse or phrase do I want to remember and think about today?

4) What did I read today that I want to share with someone else?

_____

_____

_____

_____

_____

"Lord teach us to pray"

> *Our Father in heaven, hallowed be your name.*
> *Your kingdom come, your will be done,*
> *on earth as it is in heaven. Give us this day our daily bread,*
> *and forgive us our debts, as we also have forgiven our debtors.*
> *And lead us not into temptation, but deliver us from evil.*

1) Pray for God's priorities first.
2) Pray for your needs: Provision and Forgiveness.
3) Pray for the strength to forgive others.
4) Pray for the strength to overcome temptation.

Time / Plan for tomorrow:

Symbol Study

Congratulations on making it through the first 14 days of *Come and See*! So far you have read about the introduction of Jesus, the call of his early disciples, and the beginning of his public ministry.

The next exploration method you will use is called the symbol study. It is similar to the last method in that it asks you to question the text. Not every passage will have something about each symbol, but most will if you do some digging.

Keep it up and continue to answer Jesus' invitation of Come and See!

 Write something theses verses tell you about Jesus/God.

 Write something these verses tell you about human nature.

 Write down any new discovery you have made reading these verses.

 Write down the most exciting verse in your opinion and why.

 Write anything you don't understand or want to ask about.

 Write down something these verses say you should do.

A.C.T.S. Prayer Method

It's time to learn a new pattern for prayer.

Over the previous 14 days you practiced praying the Lord's Prayer. It's important to remember that prayer is not a formula and these are just guides to help you. The new prayer guide for the next 14 days is the A.C.T.S. method. This method for prayer is not guided by specific words like the Lord's Prayer but rather organized into prayer topics. It helps you move through prayer in a way that starts with praising God and ends with asking for your own needs and the needs of others. Praying this way protects you from turning God into a Santa Clause type figure that you only go to so you can ask him for things. Here is how it goes.

Adoration: Adoration is really just worshiping God by praising who he is. It is almost like praying some lines from a worship song. Here is an example. "God, thank you for being a good God who is full of love and mercy. You created all of creation with just your voice. You are holy, powerful and loving."

Confession: Confession is going to God and asking forgiveness for your sins. It's agreeing with God that what you have done is wrong, letting go of any excuses you have for why you did it, and asking for his forgiveness. For example: "God please forgive me for yelling at my parents and disrespecting them. I confess that I was being selfish. Help me next time to honor them." This is something we need to be doing every day with God and on a regular basis with those we sin against.

Thanksgiving: This means thanking God for all he has given you. It could be for things like his love and forgiveness or it could be for your home, your family and your friends. The longer you think about what God has blessed you with, the more you realize you have to be thankful for.

Supplication: Supplication is praying for your needs and the needs of others. This is where you can pray for your friends, family and those you know who are in need. Now, after focusing on God and others, you are ready to pray for your own needs.

Hopefully this will be a helpful guide in your journey!

Jesus at the Feast of Booths

Day 15: John 7:1-24

Jesus' brothers did not believe that he was the long awaited Messiah until after his resurrection. They mockingly suggested that he go to Jerusalem for the big festival to show everyone he was a prophet. When Jesus did show up, people were amazed that he spoke with such authority since he did not study under any famous rabbis.

⬆ Write something theses verses tell us about Jesus/God:

_____

_____

_____

⬇ Write something these verses tell us about human nature:

_____

_____

_____

💡 Write down any new discovery you have made reading these verses:

_____

_____

_____

⚠ Write down the most exciting verse in your opinion and why:

_____

_____

_____

The Feast of Booths was celebrated every year in September or October. During the feast, people lived in homemade shelters covered in palm branches to remember the Israelites desert wanderings.

Write anything you don't understand or want to ask about:

Write down something these verses say we should do:

"Lord teach us to pray"

Adoration:

Confession:

Thanksgiving:

Supplication:

Your plan for tomorrow:

Can This Really Be the Christ?

Day 16: John 7:25-52

There was a great debate among the people as to whether or not Jesus was the Christ. Jesus was from the line of David and born in Bethlehem, two things that were prophesied in the Old Testament about the coming Messiah. Jesus however grew up in the small town of Galilee and not in Jerusalem. This caused many to wonder whether he was qualified to be the Messiah.

Write something theses verses tell us about Jesus/God:

_____

_____

_____

Write something these verses tell us about human nature:

_____

_____

_____

Write down any new discovery you have made reading these verses:

_____

_____

_____

Write down the most exciting verse in your opinion and why:

_____

_____

_____

? Write anything you don't understand or want to ask about:

→ Write down something these verses say we should do:

"Lord teach us to pray"

Adoration:

Confession:

Thanksgiving:

Supplication:

Your plan for tomorrow:

Woman Caught in Adultery

Day 17: John 8:1-11

The religious leaders used this woman's situation to try and trap Jesus. Jesus sees through the trap, shames those who brought the woman out, and restores her dignity by calling her "woman." The aramaic term translated was one of respect and dignity.

(↑) Write something theses verses tell us about Jesus/God:

_____

_____

_____

(↓) Write something these verses tell us about human nature:

_____

_____

_____

(💡) Write down any new discovery you have made reading these verses:

_____

_____

_____

(⚠) Write down the most exciting verse in your opinion and why:

_____

_____

_____

INTERESTING FACT:

The story of the woman caught in adultery was most likely not part of John's original Gospel. Most Bible scholars believe that it is a true story that happened during the life of Christ but are cautious about calling it Scripture.

? Write anything you don't understand or want to ask about:

_____

_____

_____

_____

→ Write down something these verses say we should do:

_____

_____

_____

_____

"Lord teach us to pray"

Adoration:

Confession:

Thanksgiving:

Supplication:

Your plan for tomorrow:

I am the Light of the World

Day 18: John 8:12-30

This is Jesus' second "I AM" statement that John records. The Pharisees continue to challenge Jesus about his claims to be the Messiah because he cannot prove them and also because he is testifying about himself. Jesus responds that God the Father testifies about him, and they don't recognize him because they don't know God the Father.

⬆ Write something theses verses tell us about Jesus/God:

_____

_____

_____

⬇ Write something these verses tell us about human nature:

_____

_____

_____

💡 Write down any new discovery you have made reading these verses:

_____

_____

_____

⚠ Write down the most exciting verse in your opinion and why:

_____

_____

_____

The Law of Moses required the testimony of two witnesses and one witness testimony was not considered valid.

? Write anything you don't understand or want to ask about:

_____
_____
_____
_____

→ Write down something these verses say we should do:

_____
_____
_____
_____

"Lord teach us to pray"

Adoration:

Confession:

Thanksgiving:

Supplication:

Your plan for tomorrow:

The Truth Will Set You Free

Day 19: John 8:31-59

The dispute between Jesus and the Pharisees continues. Jesus is continually making the point that he is the source of truth and the truth will set people free. Those who do not believe in Jesus do not know the truth and prove that they are not of God. These claims enrage the Pharisees who thought they were the ones who had special access to God.

⬆ Write something theses verses tell us about Jesus/God:

_____

_____

_____

⬇ Write something these verses tell us about human nature:

_____

_____

_____

💡 Write down any new discovery you have made reading these verses:

_____

_____

_____

⚠ Write down the most exciting verse in your opinion and why:

_____

_____

_____

John 8:58 is Jesus' clearest claim to be God. "Before Abraham was I AM." This verse greatly discredits those who say Jesus never claimed to be divine and his divinity was something his followers attributed to him long after his death.

? Write anything you don't understand or want to ask about:

_____

_____

_____

_____

→ Write down something these verses say we should do:

_____

_____

_____

_____

"Lord teach us to pray"

Adoration:

Confession:

Thanksgiving:

Supplication:

Your plan for tomorrow:

Jesus Heals a Man Born Blind

Day 20: John 9:1-41

The disciples question to Jesus about the man born blind shows the customary assumption of the day that all suffering could be traced back to individual sin. Jesus corrects this misconception and heals the man. This reaction of the Pharisees shows the true hardness of their hearts towards God. They were more concerned that Jesus healed on the Sabbath than they were amazed that a man born blind was healed.

Write something theses verses tell us about Jesus/God:

_____

_____

_____

Write something these verses tell us about human nature:

_____

_____

_____

Write down any new discovery you have made reading these verses:

_____

_____

_____

_____

Write down the most exciting verse in your opinion and why:

_____

_____

_____

? Write anything you don't understand or want to ask about:

→ Write down something these verses say we should do:

"Lord teach us to pray"

Adoration:

Confession:

Thanksgiving:

Supplication:

Your plan for tomorrow:

I am the Good Shepherd

Day 21: John 10:1-21

"I am the Good Shepherd" is one of the most well known "I AM" sayings of Jesus. Jesus is contrasting himself with the religious leaders of the day who were unfaithful shepherds to the people, caring only about their own needs. Jesus put the needs of the people before his own by giving up his life for them.

⬆ Write something theses verses tell us about Jesus/God:

_____

_____

_____

⬇ Write something these verses tell us about human nature:

_____

_____

_____

💡 Write down any new discovery you have made reading these verses:

_____

_____

_____

⚠ Write down the most exciting verse in your opinion and why:

_____

_____

_____

? Write anything you don't understand or want to ask about:

_____

_____

_____

_____

→ Write down something these verses say we should do:

_____

_____

_____

"Lord teach us to pray"

Adoration:

Confession:

Thanksgiving:

Supplication:

Your plan for tomorrow:

I and the Father are One

Day 22: John 10:22-42

Jesus is in Jerusalem for a feast. While he is there the leading Jews are pressing him to make a clear statement declaring himself to be the Christ. Jesus counters by saying that the works he has been doing are clear statements of this and again claims equality with God. After the authorities sought to arrest him, Jesus leaves Jerusalem for a more remote area where many sought him out and believed in Him.

⬆ Write something theses verses tell us about Jesus/God:

_____

_____

_____

⬇ Write something these verses tell us about human nature:

_____

_____

_____

💡 Write down any new discovery you have made reading these verses:

_____

_____

_____

_____

⚠ Write down the most exciting verse in your opinion and why:

_____

_____

_____

_____

The Feast of Dedication talked about in John 10:22 was an eight-day celebration of the rededication of the temple in December 164 BC. This holiday is still celebrated by the Jews today and referred to as Chanukah.

? Write anything you don't understand or want to ask about:

_____

_____

_____

_____

→ Write down something these verses say we should do:

_____

_____

_____

_____

"Lord teach us to pray"

Adoration:

Confession:

Thanksgiving:

Supplication:

Your plan for tomorrow:

The Death and Resurrection of Lazarus

Day 23: John 11:1-44

Jesus raising Lazarus from the dead is a turning point in the book of John. This is the final and greatest of Jesus' messianic signs he performs. This miracle is only recorded by John and through it Jesus declares himself to be "the resurrection and the life." This sign shows Jesus as both the author of life and the one who holds the keys to death. No one had ever been raised after being dead for three full days.

⬆ Write something theses verses tell us about Jesus/God:

_____

_____

_____

⬇ Write something these verses tell us about human nature:

_____

_____

_____

💡 Write down any new discovery you have made reading these verses:

_____

_____

_____

⚠ Write down the most exciting verse in your opinion and why:

_____

_____

_____

At the time of Lazarus there was the belief that the soul stayed with the body three days after death. When Martha told Jesus, "he has been dead for four days," she would have been concerned about the odor of bodily decay and also thought that it was hopeless because the soul would have left the body.

? Write anything you don't understand or want to ask about:

_____

_____

_____

_____

→ Write down something these verses say we should do:

_____

_____

_____

_____

"Lord teach us to pray"

Adoration:

Confession:

Thanksgiving:

Supplication:

Your plan for tomorrow:

The Plot to Kill Jesus

Day 24: John 11:45-57

When the Pharisees were told that Jesus raised Lazarus from the dead they resolved to have Jesus killed. They feared the people would believe he was the Messiah and lead a revolt against Rome. This could result in the temple being taken away from them and their being stripped of their autonomy. Caiaphas, the high priest, prophesied that Jesus would die so that the nation would not perish.

⬆ Write something theses verses tell us about Jesus/God:

_____

_____

_____

⬇ Write something these verses tell us about human nature:

_____

_____

_____

🔆 Write down any new discovery you have made reading these verses:

_____

_____

_____

_____

⚠ Write down the most exciting verse in your opinion and why:

_____

_____

_____

? Write anything you don't understand or want to ask about:

_____

_____

_____

→ Write down something these verses say we should do:

_____

_____

_____

"Lord teach us to pray"

Adoration:

Confession:

Thanksgiving:

Supplication:

Your plan for tomorrow:

Mary Anoints Jesus

Day 25: John 12:1-11

This passage points to the upcoming betrayal, arrest, trial and crucifixion of Jesus. It happens six days before Passover. Jesus knows his time has come and welcomes Mary's actions. The authorities are seeking not only to kill Jesus, but to put Lazarus to death as well, because on account of him many people were believing in Jesus.

⬆ Write something theses verses tell us about Jesus/God:

_____

_____

_____

⬇ Write something these verses tell us about human nature:

_____

_____

_____

💡 Write down any new discovery you have made reading these verses:

_____

_____

_____

⚠ Write down the most exciting verse in your opinion and why:

_____

_____

_____

Three hundred denarii, the amount that the perfume could have been sold for, was worth one year's wages for an average dayworker. In today's economy this bottle of perfume would have been worth around $35,000.

? Write anything you don't understand or want to ask about:

_____

_____

_____

_____

→ Write down something these verses say we should do:

_____

_____

_____

_____

"Lord teach us to pray"

Adoration:

Confession:

Thanksgiving:

Supplication:

Your plan for tomorrow:

The Triumphal Entry
Day 26: John 12:12-16

Jesus' triumphal entry into Jerusalem, where thousands came out to meet him with palm branches, is celebrated by Christians today and referred to as Palm Sunday. Word had spread among the people that Jesus raised Lazarus from the dead, and as he came into Jerusalem they hoped he would use that same power to drive out the Romans and make himself the king of Israel.

⬆ Write something theses verses tell us about Jesus/God:

_____

_____

_____

⬇ Write something these verses tell us about human nature:

_____

_____

_____

🔅 Write down any new discovery you have made reading these verses:

_____

_____

_____

⚠ Write down the most exciting verse in your opinion and why:

_____

_____

_____

? Write anything you don't understand or want to ask about:

_____

_____

_____

_____

→ Write down something these verses say we should do:

_____

_____

_____

_____

"Lord teach us to pray"

Adoration:

Confession:

Thanksgiving:

Supplication:

Your plan for tomorrow:

Jesus Predicts His Death

Day 27: John 12:27-43

Jesus is looking ahead to his upcoming crucifixion and is troubled because of what he will have to go through. This does not deter him because he was approaching the purpose for which he came, to give himself up to death to save the world from their sins. Even though Jesus performed many signs and taught among the people. Still, many did not believe in Him. This fulfilled what the prophet Isaiah prophesied about hundreds of years before.

⬆ Write something theses verses tell us about Jesus/God:

_____

_____

_____

⬇ Write something these verses tell us about human nature:

_____

_____

_____

🔅 Write down any new discovery you have made reading these verses:

_____

_____

_____

_____

⚠ Write down the most exciting verse in your opinion and why:

_____

_____

_____

Jesus fulfilled at least 20 prophecies of the prophet Isaiah, who is quoted in this passage. Isaiah prophesied nearly 750 years before the death of Christ.

Write anything you don't understand or want to ask about:

_____

_____

_____

Write down something these verses say we should do:

_____

_____

_____

"Lord teach us to pray"

Adoration:

Confession:

Thanksgiving:

Supplication:

Your plan for tomorrow:

Jesus Came to Save the World

Day 28: John 12:44-50

Jesus again declares that he is God by saying that anyone who believes in him believes in God, anyone who sees him has seen God, and anyone who rejects him rejects God. His mission was to come as the light and save people from the darkness.

⬆ Write something theses verses tell us about Jesus/God:

_____

_____

_____

⬇ Write something these verses tell us about human nature:

_____

_____

_____

💡 Write down any new discovery you have made reading these verses:

_____

_____

_____

⚠ Write down the most exciting verse in your opinion and why:

_____

_____

_____

Jesus tells his followers that he did not come to judge the world but to save the world. This is referring to his first coming. Jesus also tells of his second coming at the end of time. This coming will be for judging the world.

? Write anything you don't understand or want to ask about:

⟶ Write down something these verses say we should do:

"Lord teach us to pray"

Adoration:

Confession:

Thanksgiving:

Supplication:

Your plan for tomorrow:

Bible Study Method: Mirror Method

This section's Bible study method is called the Mirror Method. The goal is to look in the mirror of God's Word and make changes according to what you see. In the book of James were are told, "But be doers of the word, and not hearers only, deceiving yourselves. For if anyone is a hearer of the word and not a doer, he is like a man who looks intently at his natural face in a mirror. For he looks at himself and goes away and at once forgets what he was like. But the one who looks into the perfect law, the law of liberty, and perseveres, being no hearer who forgets but a doer who acts, he will be blessed in all his doing."

The Word of God is supposed to change us. If you read through the whole book of John and it doesn't change you in some way, you have missed the point. This section is all about application.

Look: Write down all this passage teaches you about Jesus and implies about his character.

Observe: How do you see yourself in comparison to Jesus? How closely does your life and character line up with the life and character of Jesus?

Change: What specific changes do you need to make in order to make your "reflection" look more like Jesus'? How can you avoid just being a hearer of the Word?

Future: How would your life change if you were able to, through the help of the Holy Spirit, make your reflection look more like Christ?

Prayer Method:

Jesus Make Me More Like You

This prayer method is simple. It is a prayer asking for change and a cry of dependence. Pray for what you wrote down in the "change" portion of your study. You cannot make any changes of spiritual significance on your own, God has to work in you. You will be given a blank space to write out your prayers based on what the passage revealed to you. For example, lets say you read John 13 and learned that Jesus is our great example of humility, but you yourself struggle with pride. Your prayer could be, "Jesus please make me humble like you and willing to serve. The mirror of your Word has revealed how selfish I am. Please change me so that my character looks more like yours."

Jesus Washes His Disciples Feet

Day 29: John 13:1-20

Chapter 13 begins the second major section of John's Gospel with the account of Jesus washing the disciples feet. This was a final proof to his disciples of his love for them and a demonstration of his humility and sacrificial love. He set this act of humility apart as a pattern for his disciples to follow. If as the Messiah could lower himself to perform the humble task of washing their feet, then they could serve others with the same humility.

>> LOOK

>> OBSERVE

>> CHANGE

≫ FUTURE

"Jesus make me more like you"

Your plan for tomorrow:

Betrayal, Love, Denial
Day 30: John 13:21-38

As Jesus reclines with his disciples while celebrating the Passover meal he tells them that one of them will betray him. After Judas departs, Jesus tells his disciples that their defining quality should be love for each other. He then predicts that Peter will deny him three times.

>> **LOOK**

_____
_____
_____
_____

>> **OBSERVE**

_____
_____
_____
_____

>> **CHANGE**

_____
_____
_____
_____

≫ FUTURE

_____

_____

_____

_____

_____

_____

"Jesus make me more like you"

Your plan for tomorrow:

I Am the Way

Day 31: John 14:1-14

This passage is often sighted as the strongest instance of Jesus' claims to exclusivity. Jesus is not saying he is A way to God, but that he is THE ONLY way to God. Even more shocking to his disciples is the claim that whoever has seen him has seen God the Father.

≫ LOOK

≫ OBSERVE

≫ CHANGE

It was customary for a man to leave his soon to be wife to build a dwelling for their new life together after marriage.
Jesus uses this with his disciples as a metaphor for Heaven when he says, "behold I go to prepare a place for you."

≫ FUTURE

....

_____

....

_____

....

_____

....

"Jesus make me more like you"

Your plan for tomorrow:

Jesus Promises the Holy Spirit

Day 32: John 14:15-31

Jesus tells his disciples that he is about to leave them and they are unsettled. He assures them that he will not leave them alone and promises the Holy Spirit. In this passage we see the entire Trinity (God the Father, the Son, and the Holy Spirit) together. Jesus also stresses the link between love and obedience.

» LOOK

» OBSERVE

» CHANGE

» FUTURE

"Jesus make me more like you"

Your plan for tomorrow:

I am the True Vine

Day 33: John 15:1-17

Jesus uses the imagery of a vine and its branches to teach his disciples about the type of relationship he wants with them. A branch's purpose is to bear fruit and it can only do that when it is attached to the vine. In the same way a Christian's goal is to bear spiritual fruit, and that can only happen when a person is connected to Jesus. Fruit bearing is proof that one is a follower of Jesus and loves him.

>> LOOK

>> OBSERVE

>> CHANGE

» FUTURE

"Jesus make me more like you"

Your plan for tomorrow:

Prepare to be Hated

Day 34: John 15:18-27

Jesus is preparing his disciples for what's to come. They should prepare to be hated and despised by many because Jesus himself was hated and despised. Those who are rejected for Jesus' sake should take heart in knowing they are following in the footsteps of their master.

>> LOOK

_____

_____

_____

_____

_____

>> OBSERVE

_____

_____

_____

_____

_____

>> CHANGE

_____

_____

_____

_____

_____

» FUTURE

_____

_____

_____

_____

_____

_____

"Jesus make me more like you"

Your plan for tomorrow:

The Work of the Holy Spirit

Day 35: John 16:1-24

Jesus is explaining to his disciples the future work of the Holy Spirit. It is actually to their advantage that Jesus leaves them because instead of God being with them He will now dwell in them. The Holy Spirit is called the Helper who will give them joy, convict the world of sin, guide them in all truth and glorify Jesus.

≫ LOOK

≫ OBSERVE

≫ CHANGE

» FUTURE

_____

_____

_____

_____

_____

"Jesus make me more like you"

Your plan for tomorrow:

Jesus Has Overcome the World

Day 36: John 16:25-33

Jesus is continuing to let his disciples know what to expect. He will soon be crucified and 40 days after his resurrection will return to his Father in Heaven. Jesus also predicts that all of his disciples will scatter and leave him in his hour of biggest need on the cross. He will not be left all alone because of his relationship with the Father.

≫ LOOK

≫ OBSERVE

≫ CHANGE

» FUTURE

"Jesus make me more like you"

Your plan for tomorrow:

Jesus' Prayer

Day 37: John 17

This is the final public prayer of Jesus recorded in John and is commonly referred to as the High Priestly Prayer. In it Jesus is giving an account of his public ministry to God the Father. He prays first for himself, then for his disciples, and ends by praying for those who would come to believe in him through the words of his disciples.

» LOOK

» OBSERVE

» CHANGE

»» FUTURE

"Jesus make me more like you"

Your plan for tomorrow:

Betrayal and Arrest of Jesus

Day 38: John 18:1-14;19-24

John 18 begins Jesus' march to the cross starting with his betrayal and arrest. Throughout the whole story John will continually emphasize that none of this was out of Jesus' control and was in fact all part of his plan and mission. John will highlight several Old Testament Scriptures that are fulfilled by what transpires.

» LOOK

» OBSERVE

» CHANGE

» FUTURE

"Jesus make me more like you"

Your plan for tomorrow:

Peter's Denial

Day 39: John 13:36-38; 18:15-18, 25-27

Today you are going to read about Peter's denial of Jesus. Jesus told Peter that he would deny him three times. Just before this incident Peter tried to show his loyalty and devotion to Jesus by taking on the Roman soldiers on his own. Now we see him fulfilling the words of Jesus by denying that he even knew him.

» LOOK

_____

_____

_____

_____

_____

» OBSERVE

_____

_____

_____

_____

» CHANGE

_____

_____

_____

_____

There is a good chance that Jesus was close enough to Peter when he denied him that he was able to hear him do it. Luke records Peter loudly cursing that he did not know Jesus. After this Jesus turns and looks at him, the rooster crows, and Peter runs away weeping bitterly.

≫ FUTURE

_____

_____

_____

_____

_____

_____

"Jesus make me more like you"

Your plan for tomorrow:

Jesus Before Pilate

Day 40: John 18:33-19:16

It is clear by Pilate's line of questioning that he was trying to discern if Jesus constituted a political threat. When Pilate was satisfied that he was not a political threat he sought to release him. The crowd instead wanted Pilate to release Barrabas, who ironically was a political threat. Pilate tried to pacify the Jews in several different ways, but in the end gives in to their demands and sentences Jesus to death by crucifixion.

» LOOK

_____

_____

_____

_____

_____

» OBSERVE

_____

_____

_____

_____

_____

» CHANGE

_____

_____

_____

_____

_____

Jesus was sentenced to be crucified and put on the cross around the same time that the Passover lambs were beginning to be sacrificed in Jerusalem. John points this out to re-affirm that Jesus was the once-for-all Passover lamb for the world.

» FUTURE

_____

_____

_____

_____

_____

_____

"Jesus make me more like you"

Your plan for tomorrow:

Bible Study Method:

Lectio Divinia (Divine Reading)

For the last five days you are going to participate in something called "Lectio Divinia" which means "Divine Reading." It is an ancient practice of reading Scripture slowly and repeatedly, allowing the words to really soak in. While reading and thinking about God's Word you also pray and ask God to let certain parts of His Word will stick out to you.

1. Read the passage through slowly and completely. Put yourself in the story. What would it be like to be there? What would you be feeling?

2. Read through the passage slowly one more time. What word, phrase, or part of it stuck out to you? Write it down.

3. Read it through a third time. Why do you think that word or phrase stuck out? Take a few minutes in prayer and ask God to reveal why it stuck out to you.

4. What does God want you to do about it? Is God asking you to make any sort of change in your life because of what you read?

The Crucifixion and Burial
Day 41: John 19:17-42

*The crucifixion of Jesus is the climax of John's Gospel and all of Scripture.
The Son of God ends up dying on a cross like a common criminal. John goes out
of his way to show how this was not a random accident and was the fulfillment
of many different Scriptures concerning the Messiah. He also goes out of his way
to show that Jesus really died, was taken down from the cross
by well know people, and buried in a known tomb.*

1) Read the passage through completely, slowly. Try and put yourself in the action. What would it be like to be there? What would you be feeling?

_____

_____

_____

_____

_____

2) Read the passage through again. What word, phrase, or part of the passage jumped out to you? Write it down.

_____

_____

_____

_____

_____

3) Read it through a third time. Why do you think that word or phrase popped out? Take a few minutes in prayer and ask God to reveal why it stuck out to you.

_____

_____

_____

_____

_____

John quotes from Psalm 22 several times in this passage. Psalm 22 is the most quoted Psalm in the New Testament and includes Jesus' famous words on the cross, "My God, my God, why have you forsaken me?" Psalms 22:15-18 was written around 1,000 years before the crucifixion but is amazingly accurate in depicting the sufferings of Christ on the cross.

4) What does God want you to do about it? Is God asking you to make any sort of change in your life because of what you read?

_____

_____

_____

_____

"Jesus make me more like you"

Your plan for tomorrow:

The Resurrection

Day 42: John 20:1-28

Mary Magdalene went to the tomb early on Sunday morning with some other woman to complete the burial process for Jesus. They were not able to complete it on Friday because of the timing of his crucifixion and the upcoming Sabbath. She was as shocked as everyone else to see the tomb empty and initially did not recognize Jesus when she encountered him.

1) Read the passage through completely, slowly. Try and put yourself in the action. What would it be like to be there? What would you be feeling?

_____

_____

_____

_____

_____

2) Read the passage through again. What word, phrase, or part of the passage jumped out to you? Write it down.

_____

_____

_____

_____

3) Read it through a third time. Why do you think that word or phrase popped out? Take a few minutes in prayer and ask God to reveal why it stuck out to you.

_____

_____

_____

_____

4) What does God want you to do about it? Is God asking you to make any sort of change in your life because of what you read?

_____

_____

_____

_____

_____

"Jesus make me more like you"

Your plan for tomorrow:

Jesus Appears to His Disciples

Day 43: John 20:19-31

Jesus appears to his disciples after his death and they put their faith in him. Thomas was not there and did not believe, but a later encounter with Christ changed his mind. John then reveals the purpose for which he wrote his book. *"Now Jesus did many other signs in the presence of the disciples, which are not written in this book; but these are written so that you may believe that Jesus is the Christ, the Son of God, and that by believing you may have life in his name."*

1) Read the passage through completely, slowly. Try and put yourself in the action. What would it be like to be there? What would you be feeling?

_____

_____

_____

_____

_____

2) Read the passage through again. What word, phrase, or part of the passage jumped out to you? Write it down.

_____

_____

_____

_____

_____

3) Read it through a third time. Why do you think that word or phrase popped out? Take a few minutes in prayer and ask God to reveal why it stuck out to you.

_____

_____

_____

_____

_____

Jesus' resurrection on Sunday is what caused the early followers of Christ to change their day of worship from Saturday to Sunday.

4) What does God want you to do about it? Is God asking you to make any sort of change in your life because of what you read?

_____

_____

_____

_____

_____

"Jesus make me more like you"

Your plan for tomorrow:

Jesus on the Beach

Day 44: John 21:1-19

After Peter betrays Jesus he goes back to fishing. Jesus meets him on the beach and a touching moment ensues. Peter denied Jesus three times and now Jesus asks him to affirm his love and commitment to him three times. Jesus commissions Peter in a scene that is reminiscent of his original calling. Peter responds to Jesus' call of "Follow Me" knowing that it would eventually cost him his life.

1) Read the passage through completely, slowly. Try and put yourself in the action. What would it be like to be there? What would you be feeling?

_____

_____

_____

_____

_____

2) Read the passage through again. What word, phrase, or part of the passage jumped out to you? Write it down.

_____

_____

_____

_____

_____

3) Read it through a third time. Why do you think that word or phrase popped out? Take a few minutes in prayer and ask God to reveal why it stuck out to you.

_____

_____

_____

_____

_____

4) What does God want you to do about it? Is God asking you to make any sort
of change in your life because of what you read?

_____

_____

_____

_____

_____

"Jesus make me more like you"

Your plan for tomorrow:

Jesus and John - The End
Day 45: John 21:20-25

The Gospel of John ends with Peter asking Jesus what will happen to John. John wrote his Gospel around the year AD 90 and at the time he was the only one of the original disciples left. There was much to write as he looked back on the life of Jesus, but he only wrote what the Holy Spirit guided him to write for the purpose of bringing people to faith.

1) Read the passage through completely, slowly. Try and put yourself in the action. What would it be like to be there? What would you be feeling?

_____

_____

_____

_____

_____

2) Read the passage through again. What word, phrase, or part of the passage jumped out to you? Write it down.

_____

_____

_____

_____

3) Read it through a third time. Why do you think that word or phrase popped out? Take a few minutes in prayer and ask God to reveal why it stuck out to you.

_____

_____

_____

_____

John was the only one of the 12 disciples to die of old age and his younger brother James was the first of the disciples to be martyred. Sometime before AD 70 John moved to Ephesus, which is in modern day Turkey. He was exiled to an Island called Patmos at the order of the Roman Emperor Domitian and it is there he wrote both his Gospel and the book of Revelation.

4) What does God want you to do about it? Is God asking you to make any sort of change in your life because of what you read?

_____

_____

_____

_____

_____

"Jesus make me more like you"

Your plan for tomorrow:

Conclusion

Now that you have finished *Come and See*, what did you find? If Jesus asked you the same question he asked Peter, "Who do you say that I am," how would you respond?

John wrote his Gospel for the purpose of those who read it coming to faith in Christ and having life in his name. Have you come to see that Jesus is the long awaited Savior, the Christ who came to take away the sin of the world? Are you ready and willing to admit that you must be born again? That is God's greatest desire for you.

If that is you and you have decided to trust Jesus as your Savior and Lord, then it is just the beginning. Jesus' next call to you is this, "Come and Follow Me."

Following after Jesus and becoming his disciple is not a one-time decision. It is an adventure that changes the course of your life. Do not enter into this commitment lightly because it will cost you everything. Jesus says, "Whoever will try and save his life will lose it, but whoever will lose their life for me will save it." It's a high calling, but one that's worth it because the one who requires that you give up your all to follow him has already given up his all so you can know Him.

Come and See. Now Come and Follow Me.

Works Cited

[1] Crossway ESV Study Bible. Wheaton, IL. 2008. ESV Study Bible Notes on John 1:1, ESV Cross Reference System, 2008.

[2] ESV Study Bible Notes on John 4:46.

[3] ESV Study Bible Notes on John 6:9.

[4] ESV Study Bible Notes on John 7:52.

[5] ESV Study Bible Notes on John 9:14.

[6] ESV Bible Study Notes on John 13:1-17.

[7] http://www.gordonconwell.edu/resources/documents/WCT_Martyrs_Extract.pdf

[8] ESV Study Bible Note on John 18.

WE ARE
THE CHURCH
GRACE COMMUNITY YOUTH MINISTRIES

**A Discipleship Resource of
Grace Community Youth Ministry**

Created by Albie Powers